OVERCOMER

STACEY-ANN SPENCE

Copyright © 2020 Stacey-Ann Spence.

All rights reserved. No part of this book may be used or reproduced by any means, graphic, electronic, or mechanical, including photocopying, recording, taping or by any information storage retrieval system without the written permission of the author except in the case of brief quotations embodied in critical articles and reviews.

This book is a work of non-fiction. Unless otherwise noted, the author and the publisher make no explicit guarantees as to the accuracy of the information contained in this book and in some cases, names of people and places have been altered to protect their privacy.

WestBow Press books may be ordered through booksellers or by contacting:

WestBow Press
A Division of Thomas Nelson & Zondervan
1663 Liberty Drive
Bloomington, IN 47403
www.westbowpress.com
1 (866) 928-1240

Because of the dynamic nature of the Internet, any web addresses or links contained in this book may have changed since publication and may no longer be valid. The views expressed in this work are solely those of the author and do not necessarily reflect the views of the publisher, and the publisher hereby disclaims any responsibility for them.

Any people depicted in stock imagery provided by Getty Images are models, and such images are being used for illustrative purposes only. Certain stock imagery © Getty Images.

Scripture quotations marked NIV are taken from The Holy Bible, New International Version®, NIV® Copyright © 1973, 1978, 1984, 2011 by Biblica, Inc.® Used by permission. All rights reserved worldwide.

Scripture quotations marked NKJV are taken from the New King James Version®. Copyright © 1982 by Thomas Nelson. Used by permission. All rights reserved.

Scripture quotations marked KJV are taken from the King James Version.

Scripture quotations marked ESV taken from The Holy Bible, English Standard Version® (ESV®), Copyright © 2001 by Crossway, a publishing ministry of Good News Publishers. All rights reserved.

ISBN: 978-1-9736-9826-5 (sc)
ISBN: 978-1-9736-9825-8 (e)

Print information available on the last page.

WestBow Press rev. date: 7/31/2020

CONTENTS

Dedication vii
Acknowledgements ix
Foreword..xi
Introduction xiii

Chapter 1   Childhood 1
Chapter 2   Migration 8
Chapter 3   Health 14
Chapter 4   Faith 23
Chapter 5   Ministry... 33
Chapter 6   Relationship 46
Chapter 7   Restoration....................................57

About the Author 69

DEDICATION

I would like to dedicate *Overcomer* to every woman who has overcome obstacles or is on her way to overcoming obstacles. I also dedicate this book to all the women who desire a path forward into all that God has destined for their lives.

To my parents—Rupert and Vertel—my six siblings—Dale, Ainsworth, Tammica, Jerome, Samantha, and Natacia—my nieces—Daliisha, Kenneice, Kaylee, Amiyah, Shania—and my nephews—Raeshawn, Dailan, Aiden, and Isaiah—you are all my family, and I love you dearly. You have taught me what matters most in life and have given me the reasons to be all that I am. Thank you!

To my friends who have encouraged me, prayed for me, and challenged me, I will always be grateful for your unwavering love.

To my readers, as you turn the pages, my prayer is that God will bring healing in every area of your life, and that any heaviness that weighs you down will be lifted. I pray that any affliction will cease, and that you will find strength in the blood of the Lamb to be an overcomer.

ACKNOWLEDGEMENTS

For the development of this book, I feel a deep sense of gratitude to the following:

- My parents, Rupert and Vertel, who have encouraged and pushed me to go after my dreams. Mom, your devotion to the Lord and your consistent prayer and love inspires me to pursue and maximize my potential.
- My siblings, Dale, Ainsworth, Tammica, Jerome, Samantha, and Natacia, and my sisters-in-law, Andrea and Anique, you have all been there for me.
- Audrea, Althea, Claudine, and Gillian, you have been there for me through ups and downs. You have been consistent, from the first moment we met. I love and appreciate each of you. Thank you for the gift of friendship for eighteen years and counting.
- Elsa, you are a gift from God. I am profoundly grateful for your encouragement and prayers. You pushed me to walk in my purpose, without wavering.

- Natasha T, Denise, Grace, Roxanne, Marlene, Michelle, Natasha P (Blue Image Group), and Jeannette, I am grateful for your encouragement and prayers.
- Kerri Ann of Conclusio House, thank you for going above and beyond just editing. Your role throughout this process was very influential, and I am beyond grateful for your contribution.

FOREWORD

In the summer of 2018, when Stacey-Ann called and told me she was writing a book, my immediate response was "Yes!" Very soon thereafter, I informed her that I would be writing the foreword.

Stacey-Ann is a fiercely loyal, faithful, and sacrificial friend. Many of you reading this book know some aspects of her story, her character, and her vivacious faith in God. As you read the following pages, it is my prayer that you will understand what she has been through, who God has called her to be, and, most importantly, how He has used her circumstances, her struggles, and her relationships to form and continue forming her into His image.

"And [Stacey-Ann] overcame him by the blood of the Lamb and by the word of [her] testimony, and [she] did not love [her life] to the death." (Revelation 12:11 NKJV)[1]

Stacey-Ann's decision to transparently document and disclose her testimony was made with great trepidation and care. This book is the outcome of her obedience to the Lord. In writing this book, she has undergone the final

---

[1] http://bible.com/114/rev.12.11.nkjv [emphasis & paraphrase added]

stages of her metamorphosis. She is now radically and forever changed. She has emerged from this process with a keen understanding of who she is, what God has done for her, and, most importantly, what He has done within her.

Observing Stacey-Ann as she wrote, rewrote, and revised each section of this book reaffirmed for me the benefit of daily journaling and daily devotions. Our journals provide keen snapshots of what we believe, as well as specific events, as they transpire. Stacey-Ann's journals are a critical foundation on which this book rests. The process of reviewing her journal, prayerfully revisiting past experiences, and inviting the Holy Spirit to reveal and heal has resulted in her fulsome restoration.

So let me introduce, or re-introduce, you to my dear friend, Stacey-Ann Spence.

Sincerely,
Natasha Toney

INTRODUCTION

I never imagined writing a book, much more sharing my testimony with individuals in a public setting, for the world to see. That all changed on Friday, July 27, 2018, as I laid in bed reflecting on my life and experiences. The thought came to my mind that I should write a testimonial for women who may have gone through similar experiences. As I shared my thoughts with two of my friends, I did so thinking that the book would happen down the road, not realizing that I needed to start the process right then.

That same evening, I felt impressed that I should start writing, but I dismissed it. On Saturday of the same week, I was nudged again to write, but I dismissed it with the decision to begin writing on the Sunday. And, as you can guess, the same nudge came again on Sunday. However, at this point, I could no longer ignore it, so I took my notebook and started writing.

So here I am on a journey to share my life, my experiences, my testimony. I believe most women in society, whether young, old, single, married, divorced, or widowed, can identify with some areas of my story. My prayer while you go through the pages of this book is that my testimony will bring you hope, encouragement, and strength to persevere through whatever situation or circumstance you are currently navigating in your life.

Remember that God is the author of your life, and He knows the beginning from the end. Just continue to hold on to God's promises, even when you do not comprehend His plan or see any way out when you go through difficult days. Keep walking and believing He will take you through. You do not need to understand His plans, but you can rest assured, knowing that it is bigger and far better than what you can see now. I hope my testimony will help you through a seemingly hopeless time, impart faith, give encouragement, and renew your strength to push forward in God. Through our testimonies, we allow God to define who we are, shape and mold us into His image, and propel us into our destiny.

CHAPTER 1
CHILDHOOD

"Children are a heritage from the Lord, offspring a reward from him." (Psalms 127:3 NIV)

I was born in the spring of 1977, in the parish of St. Mary, in the tropical island of Jamaica. My parents, Rupert and Vertel, lived together until I was about five years old, after which my dad moved to another parish for employment. He would come home on weekends, or I would go to the city when I was on break from school to spend weekends and holidays with him. Although I did not live with my dad, he played an active role in my life. Visiting with my dad was always an exciting time.

My parents got married when I was a teenager. I spent most of my childhood being raised by my mother, with my four brothers. My father was never a disciplinarian, no matter what I did. My mother, on the other hand, was the stern one. She was never afraid to discipline me and my brothers. I enjoyed being around my parents.

Most of my childhood was spent in a household with

three brothers, until my younger brother was born. I was twelve years old when my younger brother entered the scene. It was a happy time. My brothers and I enjoyed being around our baby brother, and we would help my mother with him, whether she needed our assistance or not. When she had to work, my brothers and I would pick him up from the babysitter and take care of him until she came home. Having a younger sibling in the home strengthened our interactions. We all wanted to be around him with each chance that presented itself. As older siblings, we ensured that my younger brother lacked nothing. I remember the days when my mother would give my younger brother tea to drink, which he did not like. He was not allowed to play until he drank it all, so I would always drink his tea for him so he could go and play. My brothers and I cared for our younger brother with pride and joy.

I had a good childhood. My parents could not afford to give me everything, but they ensured that my siblings and I had the necessities to keep us comfortable. We lived in a two-bedroom apartment with one washroom, a kitchen, a dining room, a veranda, and a back porch. We had electricity and running water, but not consistently. So we usually stored water in barrels for the days when there was no water in the pipe. Many days we had to fetch water from the community pipe. At times, the community pipe had no water either, so my family and I had to go to the adjoining neighbourhood to fetch water. My mother did not own a car; therefore, our means of transportation was the bus. Taking the bus daily for school was not something we could afford, so my brothers and I had to walk to school. The distance from home to school was approximately three miles. However, that was not an issue for my siblings and me, because in our community, walking to school was the norm for most of the children. That did not take away from my overall great experience in childhood. It was fun to walk to school, even when it was raining. I made the best of what I had.

I respected and appreciated what my parents sacrificed to give me the best, based on what they had. My parents and my brothers were my world. We knew how to appreciate the little that we had, and we lived our lives to the fullest. I have fond memories of growing up with my brothers. We had a special, unbreakable bond. As their only sister at the time, they looked out for me. They did not treat me any differently; I was like one of the boys in their midst. There were days when we played games outside, climbed trees, and did silly things that would sometimes get us into trouble with our mother.

I can remember how shy I was as a child. My mother told me that my shyness started from approximately age three and ended around age eleven or twelve. My mother made references to how difficult it was to even get me to participate in taking pictures at church or for the extended family visiting from Canada. That may be surprising to those who know me now, and who know how outspoken I am. Looking back, I think I was a selective mute—I only spoke when I was required to. At some point, I changed and became a very outspoken teenager. My mother told me that my outspokenness started after I began high school, around age twelve. I was no longer afraid to express my feelings or show my emotions. I was not only outspoken on the playground, but also in the classroom. I was never too shy to voice my opinions to teachers or adults, letting them know I did not agree with one decision or another. Being outspoken at school did not always work in my favour, however. There were days when I would get in trouble and would need to apologize to my teachers. I remember one incident where I was extremely outspoken to my teacher. The punishment I received from the principal was that I had to apologize to the teacher each morning for five days, after morning devotion. I didn't think it was a fair consequence, and so I gave the apology once, and decided I was not going to do it four more times. Therefore, I made sure I was late for school every morning thereafter. Suffice to say, it only led to further consequences. Some days, I wonder how my mother had the patience to deal with me as a teenager.

Having been raised in a house full of boys, I found it a little awkward whenever I was forced to interact with girls. I thought girls were too mean and catty. In high school, as my interaction with females increased, I became more aware of my appearance and took an interest in sewing. I was able to manipulate my uniforms by tailoring them to fit better. I started to design and sew clothes that I would wear to church with one of my childhood friends. Some of our designs were blazers, dresses, and skirts. Around this time, I also developed an interest in baking. I was always around my childhood pastor's wife, learning how to bake and decorate cakes and other treats.

Summers were the best time for my brothers and me. We would spend most of the summer holidays with my maternal side of the family. Spending time with my grandparents, cousins, aunts, and uncles was something we would look forward to. Most of my mother's relatives were farmers, so it was a pleasure to help them with the animals on the farm, and help with the work preparation that was involved in going to the market to sell the produce. I have some great memories spending time with my older cousins. I was able to stay out late with them, while they played games or socialized with their friends and visited the river for an evening bath.

I would spend the remainder of the summer holidays with one of my aunts on my paternal side. I enjoyed visiting her, because that was also a time to see my father, cousins, and an uncle. My uncle would take my cousins and me to the beach early Saturday mornings for about two hours before our day started. That was always something to look forward to. We would make sure we were up and ready to go, so he would not leave us behind. Spending time with my aunt was always great for me. We looked so much alike; I was like her twin. She treated me like a daughter, and I lacked nothing whenever I spent time with her.

In the summer of 1994, I graduated from high school in Jamaica. My mother did not make any preparations for me to continue my schooling the following September, because, at that point, we knew I would be migrating to Canada by the end of the year. My father had migrated to Canada in 1992, and decided to sponsor his family. He thought this was the best way for the family to have a better life. Due to our ages, he had to sponsor my brother and me right away, before we reached the age where he could no longer sponsor us. Therefore, the sponsorship came through for me and my older brother first. My brother migrated the summer of 1994, and I followed in the fall of 1994.

MY LIFE LESSON

- As adults, it is important to look back on our childhood and be grateful — I had a good childhood. My parents could not afford to give me everything I desired, but that did not take away from my overall great experience in childhood.
- Being raised with boys impacted the dynamics of my female friendships — I was raised in a household with my mother and four brothers. My daily interactions and outdoor playtimes were with my brothers.
- The love and bond between the members of my family are unbreakable — I had a good childhood, with fond memories, growing up with my brothers and parents. We had a special, unbreakable bond.
- Your story is your story — I had a great childhood with my parents and brothers.

REFLECTION

1. What are some of your fondest childhood memories?
2. Do you have the same interests as an adult as you had as a child?
3. Has your upbringing impacted your adult relationships? If yes, how?

PRAYER

Lord, I thank you for my parents and all that they have been through to provide a home for me and my siblings. You are a good Father who has protected and guarded me. *"I will give thanks to you, Lord, with all my heart; I will tell of your wonderful deeds"* (Psalm 9:1 NIV), in Jesus' name. Amen.

CHAPTER 2
MIGRATION

"For I know the plans I have for you, declares the Lord, plans to prosper you and not to harm you, plans to give you a hope and a future." (Jeremiah 29:11 NIV)

I migrated to Canada in the fall of 1994. To be frank, I was not excited about moving to Canada. The thought of leaving my mother and three of my brothers behind in Jamaica left a void in my heart, so it was very hard for me to embrace living in Canada. Upon my arrival, I was excited to see my father and my older brother, which gave me some comfort, but I missed my mom and younger siblings. As I left the Toronto Pearson International Airport, I was greeted by a gust of frigid, frosty air. I thought I would not survive a day here. I was not used to the cold, harsh winter temperatures, and I had a hard time adjusting to the cultural changes. A year later, my mother and my other brothers arrived in Canada.

I was excited to experience snow for the first time, and thought it was a beautiful sight. Still, my first Christmas in Canada was not as exciting as it was in Jamaica. Although I spent time with my extended family, it was nothing compared to the celebration that took place in Jamaica. Christmas in Jamaica was totally different from Christmas in Canada. In Jamaica, Christmas was many children's favourite time of the year. On Christmas Eve, we had what was called Grand Market Night. Most of the stores and markets, as well as street-side vendors, remained open all night. Children came out to buy their gifts, and could stay out late. The streets were blocked by people shopping, drinking, and having fun. There were fireworks, which were also very different from fireworks in Canada. Fireworks in Jamaica consisted of star lights and firecrackers. People played music and games on the streets all night, until daylight. Our family did not have all the excitement of buying and exchanging gifts like most families, but we thoroughly enjoyed staying out late and enjoying the fireworks.

My first Christmas in Canada was an emotional one. It was the first time I would spend Christmas away from my mother and three brothers. It was exhilarating decorating the Christmas tree with my cousins and putting up decorations around the house. And I found it uncanny listening to my aunts talking to my younger cousins about Santa Claus dropping off their gifts for them while they slept. Nevertheless, I listened without sharing my thoughts, because I did not want to ruin their excitement. One of my aunts hosted Christmas dinner with all the extended families and close friends. It was exciting to meet cousins and get reacquainted with cousins I only saw when they visited Jamaica on vacation.

Christmas morning was very different from what I was used to. For as long as I could remember, attending church on Christmas morning was a tradition I partook in with my siblings and mother. That first Christmas in Canada was the first time I was not in church, and I missed not having my mother and my brothers around. I found there was lots more emphasis placed on gift giving than on the birth of Christ, which I was not accustomed to. At dinner, there was a wide variety of food for all to enjoy. We listened to music and danced, while the men played dominoes and drank their favourite drinks.

After migrating to Canada, I realized that I needed to attend high school for one year. That was frustrating, because I had already graduated from high school in Jamaica. Academically, high school in Canada was nothing compared to high school in Jamaica. It was very easy, so I had no problem excelling, even when I skipped classes. Initially, I lived in Brampton and attended high school there. Culturally and socially, it was a difficult transition for me. I did not dress like the other students, and would, at times, feel uncomfortable walking through some of the hallways of the school. I felt bullied by students of a similar social background as me, who made fun of me and called me "freshie." Eventually, I moved to Richmond Hill, which was joyous for me. The students embraced me, and I did not feel fearful or uncomfortable walking through the hallways at school. Although the school in Richmond Hill was more pleasant, my time at school was not productive. I was not learning anything new. Consequently, I skipped classes to play cards and dominoes in the cafeteria. Nevertheless, I still excelled in my coursework.

Although I enjoyed living in Richmond Hill, I found the transition from Jamaica to Canada difficult. I now had to get readjusted to living with my father, since the last time we lived together I was five years old. I was excited to be living in the same household with him, but I missed having my mother's and brothers' presence. I did not attend church as much as I would have liked, because my father did not attend church, and so there was no expectation for me to attend. Sporadically, I attended with my grandmother and aunts. Since I wasn't attending church regularly or having any personal devotional time, my relationship with the Lord was impacted. However, that all changed a year later, when my mother transitioned to Canada. Once she arrived, attending church became my weekly routine, once again.

I was excited to have all of my immediate family living under the same roof. Overall, we had a good time together. In my later teenage years and early adulthood, I found it hard to fit in, and being in a new country did not make it any easier. I wanted to find my place in life and really understand my identity. Looking back, it's hard to pinpoint the internal struggles and the emotional turmoil that I experienced, because so much happened externally—transitioning from Jamaica to Canada, the different phases of transition, getting settled in Canada, getting used to this new life and culture. I met a group of ladies in 1997, while I was still settling in. We forged a great friendship. This friendship helped me through my transition, and our friendship still exists today.

I still had a passion for sewing and baking. However, I didn't have the opportunity to enhance my skills as I would've liked, and, slowly, the sewing and baking stopped. I would occasionally alter an outfit when purchased, but I never went to the extent of sewing a whole outfit.

MY LIFE LESSON

- Changing my environment impacted my personal development.
- Sometimes the people who have the same cultural background as you are the least likely to accept you — I felt bullied by students of a similar social background as me. The students made fun of me and called me "freshie."
- Migration of any form can be extremely disruptive, and needs to be managed with great care to avoid or mitigate social or emotional difficulties. Give attention to the mental and emotional impact of migration — I had to return to high school after already graduating in my home country, and I became fearful of walking through certain hallways.
- Know God for yourself — My father did not attend church, so there was no expectation for me to attend.

REFLECTION

1. What transition have you experienced that has left an impression on your life?
2. Have you experienced a transition that was forced on you? If yes, how did you manage it?
3. If you had to go through a transition again, what would you do differently?

PRAYER

Lord, thank you for guiding me through my time of transition. Father, lead me by your great mercy. Comfort me with your presence. No matter where I find myself, you are forever present, and I thank you. *"See, I am doing a new thing! Now it springs up; do you not perceive it? I am making a way in the wilderness and streams in the wasteland"* (Isaiah 43:19 NIV), in Jesus' name. Amen.

CHAPTER 3

HEALTH

"But I will restore your health and heal your wounds..." (Jeremiah 30:17a NIV)

On a sunny day, Sunday, September 12, 2004, I had a devastating car accident on Highway 400 South, while on my way to church. I have no full recollection of what happened at the scene of the accident, but I remember flashes of what transpired and can recall what the police officer told me. Apparently, my car spun across all four lanes of Highway 400 when the accident took place. I remember seeing smoke when the car came to a complete stop, but I was not sure what was happening. I panicked, and not being able to open the driver's door did not make it any easier. I crawled out of the car through the front passenger door. I could not stand on my feet, because both of my ankles were in excruciating pain. What I did not realize, however, was that the car had come to a complete stop on the shoulder and, after exiting the car, I had begun crawling onto the highway and into oncoming traffic. When I thought I was out of danger, I stopped, and I laid there for a few seconds with my eyes closed. When I reopened my eyes, I saw three people standing over me. I remember someone was trying to move me, and I screamed out in pain. I heard when one of the individuals said, "Do not move her. I am an off-duty paramedic." Another person introduced herself as a nurse, and the third person prayed while offering comfort and reassurance as we waited for the ambulance.

The police officer who showed up at the scene of the accident took my purse to the hospital and told me that the passersby had made a circle around me to alert vehicles from a distance to stop. The police officer also told me that, based on the tire marks of my car, the car had taken a three-hundred-and-sixty degree turn before coming to a complete stop. Also, he said it was a good thing I had no passengers in the car, because it was a high possibility they would not have survived. While in the ambulance, I was so secured on the stretcher that I could not move. After arriving at the hospital, I had to complete a series of x-rays and CT scans, which showed there were no broken bones or scratches on my body. The only noticeable injury was that my right and left ankles were sprained. Oh! But then the CT scans revealed the possibility of a brain aneurysm. The doctor explained that an aneurysm is an abnormal bulge of a blood vessel, with the bulge filled with blood. I will discuss that in more detail later. Now back to the accident.

I did not understand the intensity of the accident, until I went to collect my belongings from my car. When I arrived at the storage yard, I did not recognize my car, due to the extent of the damage. The entire front was gone, and the back was crushed all the way in. At that point, I understood what the police meant when he said that if I had passengers they might not have survived. I am beyond grateful to have survived such an accident. Words cannot explain how grateful I am to God for His divine protection. It was not my time to go home yet; God still had a plan for my life. What I do know is that my accident was a blessing in disguise.

When the doctors saw on the CT scan what they suspected to be an aneurysm, they restricted the intensity of the chiropractic and physiotherapy treatment I could receive, until an angiogram was completed. I was referred to the Toronto Western Hospital Aneurysm Clinic, where I was scheduled to do the angiogram. After the procedure, I met with a team of neurosurgeons to discuss the results. They confirmed the aneurysm, but they were not sure if it had been there since birth. The neurosurgeons decided to keep me under observation. I was to complete an MRI every three to four years to study the changes in my brain.

I continued to do the MRIs, and in the summer of 2015, after a regularly scheduled MRI, I was called into the Toronto Western Aneurysm Clinic to meet with a neurosurgeon to discuss the result. The neurosurgeon explained that this type of aneurysm was extremely rare, but its appearance was suggestive of something congenital, or at least extremely long standing. He explained that he did not have extensive experience dealing with this type of aneurysm, but that the ones he encountered were never reported to have caused problems. Thus, his stance with this aneurysm would be conservative. He would not recommend any interventions, because the imaging had not changed. He concluded that he would continue to monitor me and that I would continue to repeat the MRI periodically.

Six months after the car accident, I was still experiencing excruciating pain in my lower and upper back, but my doctor and chiropractor could not determine the source of my complaint. My doctor decided to schedule a bone scan. At that appointment, the technician explained that my doctor would receive the results within a week. However, the following day, I received a call from my doctor's office requesting that I come into the office to discuss the results. My doctor told me that the findings showed that I had a recent fracture and a malignant bone tumor in my left maxilla (upper jaw). Further investigation, with dental examinations and radiographs, was recommended. When the doctor explained my diagnosis, I did not register what she was saying. I was so focused on identifying the reason why my back was hurting. It was not until after I spoke to my mother and she mentioned that this was the same illness that my aunt had before she died that I really registered what the doctor meant. I broke down in tears, and my mom looked at me, firmly and confidently, and said, "You do not have any bone cancer. Don't accept it."

I had to go through a series of tests, and with that came many fears. As a Christ follower, I knew the power of prayer, but after hearing the news, I had no clue how to pray or even what to say to God. I shared what I was going through with some friends and the pastors at my church. I remember attending a prayer conference at my church. I was so down that morning, but one of my friends who is a pastor laid his hands on me and prayed. At that moment, I felt heat leave his hands and permeate my entire body. After he finished praying, I told him what I felt and that I did not think he understood the level of anointing that he had on his life. Later that afternoon, while at the prayer conference, the guest speaker stated, "I can feel a healing anointing in this place." He asked everyone in the audience who was experiencing ailment in their bodies to place their hands on the affected areas. I didn't know where to lay my hands, so I rested it on my chest. The only thing I can remember from his prayer was his breaking and binding of all cancerous cells. I felt my knees give way, and I laid prostrate on the ground.

I still had to continue with the tests, and I remember going into the hospital one day to complete a procedure. When the results came back, my doctor called me into her office and said that she did not know what to say, but that I was a mystery. The result came back showing a decrease in bone density in the left maxilla. To this day, I have been walking in the healing power of God.

After the car accident, I was not only experiencing back pain, but I was also experiencing headaches. I was taking Tylenol 3, 30-60 mg, every four to six hours, as necessary (PRN) to relieve the pain. I was at home one day with an excruciating headache, even though I had already taken two tablets (60mg). Due to my health history and the possibility of having an aneurysm, one of my brothers called an ambulance to take me to the hospital. On my arrival, a spinal tap was performed to rule out any leaking of the aneurysm. Immediately after the first procedure was completed, the doctor apologized and said that he needed to repeat the spinal tap. He later explained that he repeated the test because, due to a curve in my spine, he did not collect enough fluids from the first tap. The doctor then referred me to another specialist to examine the extent of the curve in my spine.

My mother accompanied me to the specialist. After the examination, the specialist asked my mother if I had had any issues walking as a child. My mother told him that she did not remember me having such issues. The specialist explained to my mother that I should have had difficulty walking, based on my spine's curvature. The doctor also stated that the curve in my spine was obvious by my posture and the way in which I walked. After completing a bone scan that had been requested by the specialist, I was diagnosed with scoliosis. My doctor explained that scoliosis is an abnormal curvature in the thoracic and lumbar segment of the spine.

On Saturday, December 30, 2017, I fell down four steps. After the fall, I tried to move, but it was very difficult. I made several attempts, but even with assistance from others, I still could not move without screaming in pain. The ambulance was called, and, on its arrival, the paramedics administered pain medication to provide comfort prior to attempting to move me from the house to the ambulance. At the hospital, I did an x-ray, which showed that I had suffered a fracture to my right shoulder, chipping one of the bones. The doctor was surprised that falling down four steps had caused such an impact. After my fall, I was unable to drive, because I could not use my right arm. Consequently, I went on sick leave for one month. I perceived this fall as being a reason for me to slow down and spend more time analyzing my life and seeking the Lord. It was during this time that the Lord began to reveal certain situations, environments, and people in my life.

I am a blessed and favoured child of God. He has been gracious towards me in every aspect of my life and through every obstacle that I have faced. Through it all, I have overcome, and I am still here, stronger than before. The Lord has proven Himself as Jehovah Rapha—my healer—and I am trusting my health to Him all the days of my life.

As mentioned earlier, I considered my car accident a blessing in disguise because of all the medical issues it uncovered—a malignant bone tumor, scoliosis, and brain aneurysms. There has been no lasting impact from the malignant tumor, and my last test came back clear. However, I am still living with scoliosis and brain aneurysms. I routinely undergo tests, every three years, to assess my brain aneurysms. I continue to manage my scoliosis, but it has little impact on my lifestyle. When I look back at the emotions I felt as a result of my health journey, I feel grateful and awestruck. I could not have gone through those experiences without the grace of God, my family, and my friends who were with me during some tearful days. I constantly thank God for His healing, His protection, and His favour.

Accidents and sickness tried to get the best of me, *but* God has sustained me. He has a plan and a destiny for my life.

MY LIFE LESSON

- God protects — On September 12, 2004, I had a devastating car accident. The car was totaled, but I only sustained minor injuries.
- God is my healer — Test results showed that I had a malignant bone tumor. After praying and believing God for healing and going through several tests, the final result showed a decrease in bone density in the left maxilla. To this day, I have been walking in the healing power of God.
- God has a plan for my life — I was born with scoliosis and have been living with aneurysms that have not impacted my quality of life.
- Trust God, no matter the obstacles that present themselves — reflecting on all of my health issues, and seeing how God has protected, healed, and restored me has increased my belief that God is able to do exceeding abundantly above all that I can ask or think (Ephesians 3:20).

REFLECTION

1. What miracle or healing are you believing God to do in your life or in the life of a family member or friend?
2. Do you have, or are you aware of, a testimony related to healing? Did this healing occur instantaneously or over time, with or without medical interventions?
3. Do you have any health-related needs that you would like to pray over?

PRAYER

Lord, I know you are sovereign. I believe that you love me and that I am [or _____ is] called for your purpose. Lord, give divine wisdom to the caregivers and practitioners who are administering care to me [or _____]. Lord, help me to put all my faith and trust in your healing power. *"Heal me, Oh Lord, and I shall be healed; save me, and I shall be saved, for thou art my praise"* (Jeremiah 17:14 NIV), in Jesus' name. Amen.

CHAPTER 4

FAITH

"I have been crucified with Christ and I no longer live, but Christ lives in me. The life I now live in the body, I live by faith in the Son of God, who loved me and gave himself for me." (Galatians 2:20 NIV)

Looking back on my younger years, I always loved attending church. I believe in God, because that's what I was taught as a young child. Growing up, I spent quality time in Sunday school. At the age of twelve, I attended a church revival, accepted the Lord as my personal Saviour, and was water baptized.

Before I accepted Christ, I thought I was living a normal life. After I accepted Jesus Christ as my Saviour, I was on fire for God and was excited about the things of God. I found it difficult, however, to maintain a Christian standard of living, since most of my friends were not saved. I made choices that compromised my walk with the Lord. Reading my Bible and praying were things I did only when I attended church. There was no personal or intimate time spent praying and seeking God. In fact, I do not remember being told as a young Christian that I needed to do daily devotions. Being a Christ-follower back then meant attending church services all week long, whether it was family training hour, Bible study, youth services, or Sunday service.

When I migrated to Canada, church was no longer a priority. There were times when I attended church with my grandmother and aunts, but I did not have a relationship with the Lord. I started attending church, but not on a consistent basis, until my mom found a church much like what we were used to in Jamaica. I attended that church consistently for four-and-a-half years. I even participated in the choir and taught there as a Sunday school teacher.

A few years later, I began visiting, and eventually moved to, another church. I spent several years at this new church and actively participated in both the youth ministry and the prayer team. I had a passion to pray and intercede. I truly felt the Holy Spirit leading me. As a result, my prayer life grew, and I could see God at work in my life. It was during this time that I began to realize that the Lord was speaking to me through dreams. As I continued to seek God, I felt a shift in the vision of the church I attended. This shift had a tremendous impact on my life. I started staying home and making excuses for not attending church. Eventually, I stopped attending that church. I was very grateful to have been a part of that ministry, as my participation there taught me perseverance. I had grown spiritually and had developed a deeper understanding of my calling. That was where I began surrendering my life to God and growing in intimacy with the Lord. Functioning on the prayer team exposed me to the power and effectiveness of prayer. I do not want you to misunderstand me. My life was not perfect, but I had an eagerness and a zeal to know more about God and to grow deeper in His wisdom and knowledge. However, there were areas of struggle that I had yet to surrender, which resulted in me making some bad choices. Nonetheless, in my reflection, I could envision God working in my life.

Soon after, I moved away from the church that I had attended for several years, and I joined a group of individuals who conducted weekly Bible study and prayer meetings. Three months later, this Bible study birthed a new church, and I was one of the founding members. I was deeply involved in ministry, because there was so much to do. I had a zeal to work for God and was excited to be a part of this ministry. I began helping in different areas of ministry and later decided to dedicate my time to work with the youth, the prayer team, and helping in the finance department. I allowed church duties to occupy my life, and between being a full-time student and all these church activities, I could hardly find room for personal time with the Lord. I was physically in the church serving, but so occupied with church-related duties that I was forsaking my own spiritual growth and development.

I was putting church ministry and the needs of others ahead of my own spiritual growth and development, which resulted in stagnancy. I started to make decisions that negatively impacted my walk with God and my calling. I made decisions that led to heartbreak and frustration. In my heartbreak, I had no choice but to cry out to God for help. I am thankful that God is a merciful Father, who never leaves nor forsakes His children. The Lord came to my rescue when I sought Him with all my heart, and He brought me out of my distress. Afterwards, I purposed to glorify God in my daily activities.

In 2017, I suffered a crisis that caused me to question my faith. Throughout the year, I found myself second guessing the promises that God had declared over my life. In the summer, while away with my family in Niagara Falls, I had a pivotal moment. I left the hotel early one morning to have some alone time, because I had so many unanswered questions and so many conflicting emotions. When I looked at my circumstances and the details of my life—my faith, my journey, and my testimony—I wondered why my process was so hard. I had been faithful. I had been obedient to what He asked me to do. I was living the Christian life. I paid my tithes. I knew I was not perfect, but I served God to the best of my ability, upheld the standards of holiness, and sought God and His righteousness. Yet, somehow, things were not coming together. Why was I suffering? I could not understand why a loving God would allow me to go through the experiences that I was having. I struggled to hold on to what I believed the Lord had promised me, but I could not understand why things were falling apart. I started to ask why there were so many struggles in the Christian life. I wondered, *Do I always have to struggle? Where is God in this? What did I do to deserve this? Does God really hear my prayers? Is He true to His Word? What is my purpose? Why am I always experiencing some turmoil? Why are things so difficult for me?* At that point, I started to cry. And with tears flowing down my face, I gradually started to walk in the direction of oncoming traffic, without even realizing what was happening. I could hear car horns beeping and see people staring at me. When I finally realized what was happening, I backed out of the traffic, sat on the curbside, and broke down in tears. After sitting and crying for a few minutes, I felt some peace, and I was able to return to the hotel.

A few months later, I sought God for direction and consolation, and God, in His wisdom, revealed a situation to me. At first, I could not quite understand the revelation. But as I continued to pray and wait on understanding, it became clear that the situation was having a negative impact on my life. I had to make a conscious decision to remove myself and put greater emphasis on my mental wellbeing and my spiritual growth, so that I could stay focused on the path that God was preparing for me.

Initially, my decisions caused some confusion, but by leaning on the Holy Spirit, detoxing, and allowing the Holy Spirit to speak to me, God placed me on a faith-healing journey. For the next several days, weeks, and months, I poured myself out to God for answers and for His strength and sustenance throughout that difficult season of my life. My daily routine was work, spending all my free time in fervent prayer, and reading the Word. I spent one week in fasting and prayer, seeking God's face for answers. During that week, the Lord did some wonderful and amazing things in my life. He spoke to me and gave me clarity on certain areas of my life where I was struggling. A few weeks later, I found myself smiling, with no obvious explanation. I had not heard any good news, my life was not the way I wanted it to be, but I felt at peace. I realized that there was a difference in my life, but it did not register fully until a few days later. At that point, I knew what it meant to have true rest in God and what it meant to be content.

EXCERPT FROM MY JOURNAL ENTRY—APRIL 14, 2018

> *"The feeling I have is indescribable since Thursday, April 12. I feel so happy. I find myself smiling. I haven't felt this way in a long time. I am so happy that I took all that time to pour out my sorrows, sadness, worries, and doubts to God. I still do not have everything I desire, but I feel happy. I truly understand what it is to rest in God. God has been faithful."*

My faith-healing journey continued throughout the summer of 2018. Through prayer and fasting, the Lord spoke to me in ways I could have never imagined. He opened my eyes to things I had never dreamed of. I regained my focus, and my faith was strengthened daily. The writing of this testimony was birthed out of my time of fasting and prayer. This testimony is a miracle, because, if you truly know me, I despise writing. However, the Lord laid it on my heart that I needed to do this, and even when I tried to put it off, the Holy Spirit kept nudging me. For every challenge, He gave me a solution. I told the Lord I did not have a title. He gave me one. I did not know where to begin. He gave me seven themes and the order in which they should appear in the book.

In writing my testimony, I have been challenged in many ways, including in my faith and my desire to write certain areas of the theme. However, I was reminded of God's promises for my life, and realized that I could trust the process the Lord was taking me through, no matter the challenges, fears, and difficulties that may present themselves. A friend sent me a post on social media titled "Separation before Elevation." It reminded me that I needed to hold on to my faith, trust God, and meditate on Hebrews 11:1, which says, *"Faith is the substance of things hoped for, and the evidence of things not seen."*

I had idols, including relationships, positions, leaders, and friendships. I knew that an idol was anything that uprooted the rightful place of God in my life. For God's will to be fulfilled in our lives, He must first strip away and remove every idol, so that His will to work through us and bring us into all He has destined for our lives will germinate. That was what God did in my life. He stripped me of my idols, so that I could regain perspective and evolve through faith in Christ Jesus. My faith in Him was renewed, His directions were resurrected, and what He placed in me became alive, again. Not only was I stripped, but He also placed me in a new environment where He could propel me into what He has called me to. Building my faith in God has been a process and is something that I am still asking God to help me to do daily.

Today, I live my life in total surrender to God and His will for my life. Being obedient to His will has birthed something beautiful that I never thought was possible. I have never been so humbled before God. I ask Him daily to crucify my flesh so He can be glorified in my life. The process is hard, but it is worth doing. Struggling with my faith has prevented me from taking anything for granted and from making myself into what I am not. It has helped me to recognize that I need God in my life to keep me from losing my grip in my faith walk. It is so easy to lose grip on faith.

Sometimes the Lord needs to take us out of our comfort zones to help us to recognize our true worth and the calling that He has placed on our lives. I am grateful for the experiences and the lessons that I learned while under the various leadership I have encountered.

MY LIFE LESSON

- Being a Christian is about having a relationship with God — Knowing who He is as our creator. Reading my Bible and praying was something I would only do when I attended church. There was no personal time spent praying and getting into the Word. As a matter of fact, I do not remember being told as a young Christian that I needed to do daily devotions.
- Understanding and handling adversity — I am recognizing how the Lord can use adversity in my life to achieve growth and His purpose.
- Understand what it means to trust and have faith — Faith is a journey where we encounter circumstances that seem insurmountable, and we decide to surrender them all to God, receive

His directions, and watch Him move on our behalf. Faith is facing obstacles, remembering the promises of God, looking at past victories, and trusting God that He will do the same in each new situation.
- As Christians, our mandate is to align ourselves with God's words and be obedient. Our responsibility is to obey what God is asking us to do. His responsibility is to bring those promises to pass — In my faith journey, I have employed many tools to draw near to God, hear His voice, obey what He has asked me to do, and, as a result, come in alignment with His will.

REFLECTION

1. How do you define faith?
2. What does your faith journey look like?
3. What promises has God given you that you are still waiting to see manifested?

PRAYER

Thank you, Lord, for sustaining me when I walked through dark days with my faith. Help me to hold on to my faith when trials and temptations come my way. Help me to seek you with my whole heart. As I continue to walk with you, help me to walk in your wisdom. Give me the power and strength to tear down any stronghold in my path, in your name. Faith is the confidence in what I hope for and the assurance about what I do not see (Hebrews 11:1 NIV). *"May the God of hope fill you with all joy and peace as you trust in him, so that you may overflow with hope by the power of the Holy Spirit"* (Romans 15:13 NIV), in Jesus' name. Amen.

CHAPTER 5

MINISTRY

"Then I heard the voice of the Lord saying, 'Whom shall I send? And who will go for us?'" (Isaiah 6:8 NIV)

Christ followers are called to love God and people, and to be disciples proclaiming the Gospel. I knew my interests, my gifts, and what I was passionate about, but I never thought of turning them into ministry. I graduated from Seneca College of Applied Arts and Technology with a Diploma in Business. I completed my certification in Payroll at The Canadian Payroll Association and worked as a Payroll and Benefits Administrator for several years. After the car accident, I was unable to work for over a year. As I was transitioning back to work, I noticed that I was unable to work a nine-to-five schedule, due to the aftermath of my accident. So I decided to venture into something new. I still have a love for working with numbers, but I have developed a new desire to help others, especially females, who have experienced areas of turmoil or obstacles on their life journey. I researched programs that would fulfill my passion for helping others and decided to enroll in the Child and Youth Worker Program at Humber College, where I graduated with a Diploma. I felt this program was more in line with where the Lord was leading me. After some years working as a Child and Youth Worker, I completed my Bachelor of Arts in Child and Youth Care at Ryerson University.

As a young child, I always gravitated towards helping others. I would go above and beyond to help others, and I continue to do so today. I do not know whether I just tend to find the people that need help or they find me. At the age of fourteen, I remember working with the Sunday school director as an administrator and later getting involved in youth ministry. As I grew older, my passion to serve deepened. I served in my local church in the youth department as a camp counsellor, youth leader, and administrator. My volunteer activities extended to organizing events and filling various roles in the finance department. I truly enjoyed utilizing my skills to help the church grow. My involvement in my local church body was done with zeal and passion. Nevertheless, I felt that I had so much more to offer but never had the courage to pursue.

After many years of serving, I began to seek the Lord for direction on what to pursue in ministry. He began to reveal aspects of my calling in bits and pieces. I was at a crossroads, where I was known as the "youth events lady" and finance person, but deep inside I knew the Lord had given me a burden for women. I knew that what the Lord had placed in my heart was what He wanted me to accomplish. This burden for women later forced me to come out of my comfort zone. However, the fear of leaving that place of comfort was crippling. I served in the youth ministry and finance department for several years and flourished. As a result, the leaders and fellow volunteers felt that this area of ministry was my calling. Reflecting on my journey in life helped me to realize that I had always had the urge to serve women. As a youth leader, I developed and cultivated rich and meaningful relationships with young women. It was the work with young women coupled with my life experiences that helped to confirm my passion to pursue a ministry dedicated to helping women.

On January 18, 2016, the Lord spoke clearly into my spirit while in prayer:

> *"My daughter, arise! I have called you to do my work. Be not afraid, because I am with you. I will guide you and I will put my words in your mouth. Be strengthened. Be of good courage. I am your God. I have anointed you for such a time as this. I am with you. You will do exploits in my name. Stand firm on my promises. I have seen your tears. I know your heart. Arise, my daughter. Do not be afraid; I am with you. I will go before you. Put your fear and doubt aside. Your calling is great. I have called you to be a beacon to my daughters. Arise! Arise and stand upon my promises. I have placed a lot in you for my children. Be*

> *not afraid. Move when I say move, because*
> *I am with you. I will never leave you nor*
> *forsake you."*

At that moment, I knew what I had envisioned for my life was really what the Lord had for me. The Lord was truly speaking to me through my dreams to show me what He would use me to do for His daughters. Though I knew it was God leading me, I was often fearful and often questioned God. What did God see in me? Why me? How do I move past the way people see me? How do I navigate women and their emotions? Why would He ask me to be vulnerable, when so many women are not transparent with their experiences?

I often form a comparison between myself and Moses. Moses was an Israelite raised by Pharaoh; in contrast, I was raised by my mother, and was surrounded by my four brothers. Moses tried to make peace between two of his fellow brethren. The one who was wrong turned on him arrogantly and said, *"Who made you ruler and judge over us?"* (Exodus 2:14 NIV). Likewise, as I began building relationships with women and providing encouragement, I was criticized. At times, I was very disappointed by the behaviour of some individuals, to the point where I suffered mentally and emotionally at the hands of many. For example, I made sacrifices to attend to the needs of people whom I considered and looked up to as friends. I gave out of my need financially, and at times gave up my time to meet their needs. All I expected in return was a shoulder to lean on when I was facing adversities. I discovered later that my priorities were not important to these individuals. Moses embraced his calling with God after he removed himself from his brethren, his royal privilege, his environment, and his friends, and entered a new relationship in a new environment where he was a stranger. Similarly, I embraced my calling after I removed myself from my brethren and placed myself in a new environment with strangers.

I have always heard individuals speak about church hurt, but I never understood the depth of what it meant. Well, let's just say church hurt is very real and very painful. Fervent prayer, counselling, and divine intervention from the Holy Spirit are necessary for healing. I went through a very challenging season in my life, where I experienced church hurt. After years of walking in close relationship with my senior leaders, I experienced betrayal. I needed my church leadership's support, since, due to our relationship, they were aware of my dilemma. However, I did not receive any support via text messages or phone calls. I was left to brave my situation alone. I was hurt deeply, because I had served faithfully in that place of worship for a number of years. I supported leadership personally, and held several leadership positions. During this season, I felt alone, in spite of my years of dedication. Due to the church hurt I endured, I became very resentful of charismatic churches. I couldn't fathom how one could say they were spiritual and anointed in a church service but turn a blind eye to a hurting congregant, especially while being aware of the situation. The church is a place of healing for hurting people. Therefore, when you bring your hurts to church and the church lets you down, it compounds your pain and creates further confusion.

For a period of time, I blamed myself for being there for leadership who didn't care about me but about what I had to offer. I thought things were just not fair. Every time I think about that season, I find myself emotional, and I still can't fully believe what I experienced.

I was hurt deeply by leaders I looked up to as mentors, and that has made me extremely cautious about putting myself in a position where I am vulnerable. There were times when I found myself looking at God through the lenses of my leaders, which resulted in my hesitance to do anything related to the things of God. If my shepherds whom I could see were not able to support me, then how could I trust a God I could not see? Based on this incremental rejection, I struggled with God, church leadership, and the value people placed on me. My church hurt affected the way I communed with God, and there were days when I didn't want to speak with Him. One morning on my drive to work, the Lord, in His sovereignty, reminded me that He is not like man; He did not hurt me, so I shouldn't look at Him through the lens of men. The Lord reminded me that He has always been my loving Father. I started to embrace His love and mercy. He led me to people who embraced, encouraged, and prayed with me through that season.

I know that I'm called to do great things for the Kingdom; therefore, I continue to focus on my healing journey, on my identity, on building authentic relationships, and on being a part of a ministry that undergirds, propels, and protects me. I am fully aware that there are many good church leaders, and not all leaders can be seen through the lenses of my experience. As a result of my process, I know that God loves me. Despite the pain, He protected me and allowed me to grow through my experience.

Since then, I have decided to obey the Lord at all costs. I have embraced my calling to help women, and have purposed to fulfill the promises He has declared over me. Like Moses, I came up with many excuses to prove to God why I was not qualified to speak to women. I believe that *"He who began a good work in me is faithful to carry it on to completion until the day of Christ Jesus"* (Philippians 1:6 NIV).

Approximately two years ago, I was wrestling with the desire to work in women's ministry. I eventually decided to join the women's ministry at my local church. One Sunday while in church, I had such a strong conviction to serve in the women's ministry that I approached the leader after service to discuss my desire. She was ecstatic and declared, "This is an answer to my prayer! I asked God to send help."

Later that same year, I was asked, along with other council members, to participate in an exhortation. An exhortation in church is about giving a speech aimed at encouraging believers. I reluctantly agreed. I was experiencing a very difficult time in my life and was not clearly seeing the promises of God being fulfilled in my life. The title I chose for my exhortation was "In the Meantime, What Do You Do?" It was hard to convey the topic to the ladies while struggling with the idea that God speaks to us and tells us things that we are yet to see materialize in our lives. God said it, we heard it, we believe it. So what do we do while we are waiting? Although I went through with the exhortation, it was very difficult, because I was struggling with "In the Meantime." I had no clue what it felt like to rest and completely trust God. Nevertheless, I did the exhortation out of obedience. The exhortation was a learning experience for me. I learned that "in the meantime" means to be still and wait upon God.

In 2013, I had the desire to start a girls' group. I wrote the plans but did not move forward until the summer of 2017. I decided to start the group after speaking to an individual about her relatives' experiences. My purpose for creating a girls' group was to provide support to adolescent females who are experiencing a wide range of issues in their teenage years. The group was launched on March 17, 2018, with frequent meetings designed to empower teenage girls. The curriculum was based on a draft outline taken from my journal. The name of the group was formed during a brainstorming session with the girls. We decided to name the group E.L.L.A—Empowered, Leader, Lovely, Affirmed. The group gave an outlet to these young girls to share their experiences, and it provided the necessary encouragement and guidance they needed to follow the right path to success. It provided young ladies with the opportunity to explore their experiences as well as their strengths in a safe and non-threatening environment. Although E.L.L.A.'s group meetings are currently suspended, there are ongoing interactions and check-ins with some of the young ladies.

Over the years, I often experienced a mysterious pain whenever I was praying, or at nights while dreaming. While dreaming, I would begin to feel the onset of this pain. In 2016, the experience was happening more frequently, especially whenever I prayed about certain situations. I did not understand it, but I also could not dismiss the occurrence of pain. I reached out to different individuals for spiritual counselling, to try to understand my experiences. I did not receive anything insightful. In fact, I could sense that some of those individuals whom I sought for help did not believe me and thought something was wrong with me. I eventually concluded that I was under spiritual attack, due to the timing of the occurrences and physical sensations. One year later, I had an experience that caused me to adamantly set out to get some answers. I spoke to a close friend about my experiences, and she suggested that I call her mother and have her pray with me. I called my friend's mother—let's refer to her as Jane—and we arranged a time to meet and pray. When the date was established, I decided to fast and pray on that day. However, I heard in my spirit, "No, you are fasting for the entire week." I was off work for March break and, therefore, had the time to spend in prayer and fasting.

When I met with Jane and her husband for prayer, they read scriptures and exhorted. At that point, I realized the Lord was doing something in my life. The scriptures that were used were the same scriptures the Lord had been using to minister to me in the prior weeks. After we prayed, Jane told me what the Holy Spirit had impressed on her heart concerning my ministry. I revealed to her and her husband what I was experiencing and that I believed I was under spiritual attack. She said, "Stacey, it's the ministry that the Lord has called you to that He is birthing in you. Deliverance needs to take place. This is the reason for your encounters and why they occur at certain times."

Based on our discussions, Jane instructed me how to pray about particular issues and how to target my prayer.

I decided to follow the path on which the Lord was directing me and to embrace what He had called me to. I began to surrender myself totally to the authority of God, so that the Holy Spirit could birth what He desired to come forth. I entered a season of prayer and converted a section of my bedroom into an area for prayer. I began to post prayers on my wall and adhere to a very rigid devotional time. The Lord was transforming my life, and I started to see what He was doing through me and the people he would send my way. During that season, I would wake up at a specific time to pray specific prayers for specific people. This was done through the leading of the Holy Spirit and was confirmed by a friend who had just received a Bible teaching on the Eight Prayer Watches. As she explained, we realized the Holy Spirit was leading me to pray according to the eight watches. We were amazed. Today, I walk in the obedience of what God has called me to. Even when I feel scared, I continue to persevere while trusting the Lord. Through my obedience, I can see God at work in my life and know that His plans are bigger than my fears.

One day, I was praying with a friend and these words were spoken over my life: "From the shadows to the platform." As I write this, it is August 2018, and I can see myself emerging from the shadows. I can see where the Lord is pruning and preparing me for the work He has ahead. When I started writing my testimony, I was not sure what was going to happen, or how I would go about doing it. But now I can see this as a work of God. When I began to write this book, the Lord placed women from all walks of life in my path. I either provided encouragement or walked them through what they were encountering. I know now that there is no way I can stop what the Lord has begun in my life, as long as I walk in obedience. Obedience is allowing me to minister to women based on my own experiences and what the Lord has done in my life. I recognize that the Lord has a work for me to do and that the call on my life is great. For God to move in my life, He had to isolate me from the people and things that consumed me, so I would have no choice but to seek Him, so He could birth something beautiful out of my pain.

Isolation, in itself, is neither bad nor good. In my opinion, it's the circumstances under which isolation takes place that determine whether it is good or bad. I have experienced both negative and positive isolation. I was isolated within an environment because of how I was treated, and when the treatment continued, I removed myself so that God could speak to me about me. When I experienced three levels of betrayal, that isolation was negative. I retreated from people as a result of the trauma I encountered. I shut people out. I have also experienced positive isolation when I spent time learning to truly understand who I am. Doing so helped me to recreate my identity in Christ and refocus on what really matters. Isolation allowed me to see my value and make myself a priority. This voluntary separation caused me to spend time speaking with the Lord, which enabled me to stay positive and open to hearing the Holy Spirit. Time alone reminds me of how much I am loved by my family, and reveals my authentic relationships. During times of isolation, God reminds me of His love for me.

MY LIFE LESSON

- What do you love to do? What are you an expert at? What are you passionate about? What angers you? — These may be indicators of what you are called to do. Answering these questions will help you to identify your area of ministry.
- Seek God for your purpose in life — After many years of serving, I began to seek the Lord to confirm what He would like for me to do. He began to reveal aspects of my calling. The Lord confirmed to me on January 18, 2016 what He had called me to do.
- Trust God that when He calls you, He will equip you and provide the resources you need — As I began to write this book, the Lord placed women from all walks of life in my path. I either provided encouragement or walked them through what they were dealing with. Obedience to Christ allowed me to minister to women based on my own experiences and what the Lord has done, and is still doing, in my life.
- You must know what God has called you to do, despite what people around you say — I was known as the "youth events lady" and finance person, but the Lord had given me a burden for women. I knew what the Lord had placed within me and what He wanted me to accomplish.

REFLECTION

1. Do you know what ministry you are called to? If yes, how did you determine this?
2. What are your gifts, spiritual and/or natural? Are you actively developing them?
3. The ministry that you're called to, do you think it is permanent or seasonal? How do you know this?

PRAYER

Father, you call me your child. Continue to show me my purpose, as I seek you daily. Help me to walk into what you have called me to do. You're a faithful father who will never leave me nor forsake me. Help me to live a life that is totally surrendered to you. Align my heart to your heart, and my will to your will. God, I ask that you continue *"to do exceeding abundantly above all that [I] ask or think, according to the power that worketh in [me]"* (Ephesians 3:20 KJV), in Jesus' name. Amen.

CHAPTER 6
RELATIONSHIP

"Above all else, guard your heart, for everything you do flows from it." (Proverbs 4:23 NIV)

Relationship is a state of connection between two or more individuals. It can be hard work, but it is usually fulfilling. Looking back, I can see where relationships have affected me both positively and negatively. Positively, because relationship is an important aspect of my life, both spiritually and secularly. Negatively, because, at times, relationships have been a hindrance to my walk with God. Nevertheless, relationship is an integral part of life, whether it pertains to God, family, friends, coworkers, or one's spouse. Relationship is necessary for growth and health.

As mentioned earlier, I have four brothers and two sisters. I am the second eldest. I grew up in a household with my four brothers and my mother. Growing up, I had a good bond with my brothers. In the early 1990s, I discovered I was a part of a blended family. My father had two daughters that he did not tell me about. I met one of my sisters when she was one year old, and reunited with her when she was eleven years old. I met my other sister, who is the youngest, when she was nine years of age. I was very excited to meet them, considering I always wanted to have sisters.

Growing up, my relationship with my father was amazing. I enjoyed the time we spent together. My father has always been a part of my life; however, I did not share my secrets, my struggles, or my daily encounters with him. He worked hard and ensured that all my daily needs were met. He was not an emotional person. His love was expressed through his provision for the family. Unlike other children, I never got hugs from my dad, so I never had any expectations of him expressing his love to me with hugs and kisses. Nevertheless, I knew he loved me.

My relationship with my mother was very different. She raised me for most of my childhood. She sacrificed a lot for me in making sure I had a good education, and in meeting my daily needs. However, our relationship in my early adult years was more bittersweet. During my adulthood, my mother and I had extended rough patches, where we could not see things through the same lens. This difference of opinion would lead to many disputes. I now realize that I had my mother's temperament, which was why we saw things differently and were unable to resolve many of our disagreements. Although we bickered, my mother was, and still is, my world. Despite the issues between us, I always felt loved by her. She was never afraid to show me my faults and, at the same time, demonstrate her love for me. My mother was there for me, no matter what trials I encountered. Throughout my illnesses, when pain kept me awake during the night, she was always present at my bedside, either praying or applying warm compress to provide comfort. Nonetheless, I was never comfortable opening up to her about my experiences and my challenges. It was much easier for me to relate my challenges to my friends, simply because I did not want to disappoint her and was not prepared to accept her harsh opinions, discipline, or disappointments. Therefore, I placed rigid boundaries between us.

I am told by my friends that I am an amazing friend. I have always considered myself sensitive to the needs of others, and I frequently go out of my way to assist those in need. I consider myself strong, honest, loyal, trustworthy, caring, and straightforward. I never pretend to have all the answers. I pride myself on being there for friends, whether they are experiencing turmoil, distress, or happiness in their lives. I will go above and beyond for someone I consider my friend. I believe God has gifted me in this area of relationship.

I have come to realize that not everyone that enters my life and claims to be my friend is genuine or is meant to walk with me in certain seasons of my life. There are different categories of friendships. God has revealed to me my confidants, my friends, and my acquaintances. I have been through many betrayals and ups and downs with friends. I have reached a point in my life where I place each person in a category and, in doing so, I minimize my expectations of them.

At times, God has divinely placed friends in my life for a season, to fulfil certain purposes. Then when

I become too comfortable in those relationships, things change, forming barriers to my spiritual life. For example, I was a close friend of one of my church leaders, alongside whom I also actively volunteered. Over the course of the friendship, we endured many highs and lows, and the relationship became a kind of support for me. As the nature of our friendship changed and became more one-sided, it impacted my spiritual growth. Looking back, I can see how those leaders were unable to see the most authentic version of me and my potential. The Lord used them in the past, so they saw me as someone who endured certain things, but they did not see my growth. There were many ministry opportunities that came up, and I was overlooked and not seen as a viable candidate. I was seen through my past circumstances and not for who I was becoming. My personal relationship with my leaders provided them with details that became a hinderance to my work in ministry. As I reflect on my friendships, I have come to an understanding that friends can only give what they have, based on the capacity of their experiences. It is important to seek God when choosing friendships. I have also encountered selfish people who have used me for their own gain and self-fulfillment. Then once I no longer served their purpose, I was discarded or minimized. Do not confuse "friends" who use and abuse people for their own pleasure with those friends who are only supposed to be around for a season.

You see, there are friends that come into our lives for a reason, some are for a season, and others are for a lifetime. There are also dimensions to friendships. Over time, friendships can organically grow closer or grow more distant. In certain seasons, friends can become confidants or can become acquaintances. Sometimes there are friends who are there to walk us through a difficult time we may be experiencing, and provide direction and support. When that season of difficulty is over, and change starts to happen in the relationship, it is an indication that this season or dimension of friendship is over. When we hold on to those relationships after the season is over, we do damage to both people. Some warning signs that the season is coming to an end may include the person walking away, persistent disagreements between you and the person, or the person showing malintent towards you. If there is codependence in the relationship, then there needs to be a change in the relationship's boundaries. Over time, the reason behind the friendship may become evident, which makes it so much easier to manage.

A confidant is someone you can share your innermost desire with, knowing that it stays between you and that person. This is a person who demonstrates their consistent support of the most authentic version of you. You can discern a confidant based on your years of friendship, their response and support in times of distress, and the leading of the Holy Spirit.

I believe if you are a woman, then your best friend should not be a man. Having a best friend of the opposite sex can cause boundary issues. I had a close male friend that I could speak to about any and everything, and vice versa. Eventually, our lines got tangled. And our friendship birthed intimate feelings that eventually grew to be something that was never intended. Thank God, we went through a restorative process that has allowed us to remain friends today. We have acknowledged our faults, forgiven each other, and have moved on with our friendship, but not without putting boundaries in place. Today we encourage each other to be the best version of ourselves.

Boundaries are important in all relationships, especially male and female friendships. There are personal and relationship boundaries. For relationship boundaries, it will take work to establish and monitor each person's expectation and overall awareness. Boundaries may look different for each person and each relationship. Your boundaries should cover emotional and physical aspects, to name a few. There must be honesty and open communication between all parties. When your friend is of the opposite sex, it would be beneficial to introduce your friend to your partner to alleviate any awkwardness that may arise, and ensure your partner is comfortable with this friendship. It is also important to do frequent check-ins with your partner.

God intended friendship to involve trust, intimacy, transparency, and vulnerability. Man was not created to live alone. That was why God created Eve to be Adam's soulmate, wife, friend, and confidant (Genesis 2:22). However, in friendship we sometimes experience pain, betrayal, and misunderstanding. Nonetheless, friendship is an important part of our life's journey. People need each other. I have learned, through my many life experiences, that discernment is very important, not only in the spiritual journey but also when deciding to venture into intimate relationships and in navigating who we allow into our lives as friends. Friendship is not something that you press an on-off button to get into and get out of. Some friendships are promoted in certain seasons, and others are demoted.

My intimate relationships were the hardest section to write about. Intimate relationships are so closely tied to who we are and how we want to be seen by others. When an intimate relationship is broken, it takes a lot from an individual and may leave a feeling of loss, hopelessness, loneliness, and despair. However, when all the pain and hurt is turned over to God, and healing occurs, something beautiful can happen, because God gives total healing, peace, and joy. *"But as for you, you meant evil against me; but God meant it for good"* (Genesis 50:20a ESV).

My intimate relationships resulted in brokenness that only God could heal, from the inside out. I have been in intimate relationships where I should have lost my mind, but God has a plan and a specific design for my life. No plan of the enemy can stop my destiny. After one particular break up, I hit rock bottom, lost my joy, my peace, my identity, and almost gave up on God. But God pulled me out and reminded me that I was His child. He has called me to greatness, and He would accomplish His promises in my life. When we are going through our hard times, it is hard to see His hand at work and what He has in store for us. We tend to focus on the facts and what we see and lose hold of God's promises. We must remember that God's plan is the best for us, and it is always bigger than our present circumstances.

I have stayed longer in broken relationships than I should have, because I was more concerned about being embarrassed. My fear of what others would think crippled my ability to heed all the warning signs. I would hold on to the possibility of reconciliation. I would remain in frequent contact with my ex, and our conversations would basically be the same as when we were in a committed relationship. This gave me hope. In one such relationship, my significant other had moved on and was having an emotional relationship with another woman. When the Lord revealed what was happening between my ex and that person, I had no choice but to move on with my life and deal with the revelation and pain of what had come forth. I leaned into the Holy Spirit for comfort and peace to get through what I was feeling and experiencing. My desire for companionship and for a family of my own was so strong that it hindered my ability to seek God's directions and wisdom in this area of my life.

I've learned that a broken or unhealthy intimate relationship involves a lack of respect, trust issues, control issues, possessiveness, and manipulation. A relationship is broken when a couple no longer prioritizes each other, and interest in the relationship changes. There are certain signals that a relationship is broken. However, we often overlook those signs for several reasons—a desire for companionship, insecurities, personal brokenness, or a lack of awareness that the relationship is broken. At times, it is not until something drastic happens, and we step away, that we realize what we have subjected ourselves to.

The pain of a broken heart can be overwhelming, but you can move forward by pressing into Jesus. You can move on through prayer, trusting God for change, and counselling. As you move on, get reacquainted with who you are as a person, by pursuing a new interest and refocusing on your priorities. Doing those things can lead to the healing of a broken heart and the letting go and surrendering of your emotions and journey to God. In the past, I used relationships, watching movies, and socializing to help me ease my pain from heartbreak. However, I did not find real healing from these things; they only numbed the pain temporarily, which would lead to a cycle. This time around, I was determined to get total healing and avoid repeating the same cycle of my past. I poured out everything I was feeling to the Lord in prayer, and I removed myself from anyone or anything that would pose as a distraction for me during this time.

Reflecting on the pain and hurt that I endured in past intimate relationships caused me to focus on surrendering all aspects of my life to the Lord. It was not easy, but, eventually, it became a habit to take all my issues and requests to the Lord. Determining when and how to enter relationships was just an expression of my surrender to God. I have decided not to enter any more intimate relationships without first receiving clear directions and guidance from God.

MY LIFE LESSONS

- We forget that our parents are human and have different personalities and experiences — My father has always been a part of my life. However, I never told him my secrets, struggles, or experiences. He worked hard and ensured that all my daily needs were met. He was not an emotional person. His method of expressing love was demonstrated in his provision for the family. Consequently, in my childhood, I never had any great expectations of him expressing his love to me with hugs and kisses.

- Develop personal authenticity and grow in integrity — Be true to who you are and to the process of becoming who God destined you to be in relationship. I have always considered myself strong, honest, loyal, trustworthy, caring, straightforward, sensitive to the needs of others, and as one who never pretends to have all the answers. I pride myself on being there for my friends, whether they are experiencing turmoil, distress, or happiness in their lives. I will go above and beyond for someone I consider to be my friend. I believe God has crafted me in this area of relationship.
- Boundaries are designed to protect you — In my desire to be a great friend, I have sacrificed beyond what God has called me to do. I have been loyal to friends and relationships that have not been loyal to me.
- You need wisdom to discern who is on your side, what to say, and who covers you. Vulnerability, accountability, and environment will either kill or restore you — I have seen areas in my life restored as a result of my removing myself from certain environments and relationships.

REFLECTION

1. How do you discern the level of relationships in your surroundings?
2. Have you ever entered a relationship that hindered your growth in ministry or that killed your ministry? If yes, describe.
3. What is your perspective of a good friend? Provide examples.

PRAYER

Lord, you are a merciful Father. You are gracious and full of compassion. Lord, you are sovereign, and I surrender my heart, my control, my dreams, and my aspirations to you. God, forgive me for not seeking you the way I should with matters that concern the heart. Thank you that amidst the hurt, pain, and turmoil, you did not leave nor forsake me. God, I ask you to give me strength in this area of my life, so that I can make good and godly decisions when entering relationships. *"Oh, give thanks to the Lord, for He is good! For his mercy endures forever"* (Psalm 107:1 NKJV), in Jesus' name. Amen.

CHAPTER 7

RESTORATION

"And the God of all grace, who called you to his eternal glory in Christ, after you have suffered a little while, will himself restore you and make you strong, firm and steadfast." (1 Peter 5:10 NIV)

When I decided to share my story, I had no clue what restoration in my life would look like. I told myself I was not close to what I believed restoration looked like. I figured I would just write the other chapters of the book, and when my life transformed into how I believed restoration was supposed to look, then I would write about restoration. With many debates between myself and fear, I continued to write. It was impressed on my spirit that when I got to the topic of restoration, the Lord would reveal to me exactly what it looked like and what to write.

While spending time with the Lord, He showed me that my restoration process started on my first visit to a particular church. On that Sunday, February 18, 2018, while in worship, the Lord spoke into my spirit and said,

"Separate yourself; it is well." On February 17, I was thinking about separating myself from an environment that was no longer conducive to my growth, so when God spoke to me, He was just confirming a decision that I was trying to make. I never thought that the decision to separate myself would be the catalyst to my restorative process. I began to reflect on my journey throughout the month of February and onwards, and realized that the Lord was taking me through a process of healing and transformation.

I needed emotional healing, as a result of the threefold trauma I had experienced. The concurrent loss of a great friend and mentor, the betrayal of a friend, and the manipulation from an ex-boyfriend resulted in overwhelming emotional despair. Individually, heartbrokenness, church hurt, and betrayal was hard; but when compounded, it was excruciating. I felt shocked, then numb, then angry. I was grieving the loss of relationships and people that I truly did not know. These incidents impacted my ability to trust others and decide who I would relate to.

Throughout my healing process, the Lord impressed specific themes on my heart, such as motives, being intentional, and vindication. I realized from these themes that I needed to have the right motives to drive the right actions, which would lead to getting the right results. Being intentional meant figuring out how to separate myself, and asking myself, *What do I need to add to my life? What do I need to let go of? What do I need to focus on?* Vindication, in this sense, meant I was going to live my life to the fullest, and allow God to fight my battles in His timing, under His jurisdiction. Confident in what God had spoken, I began to surrender everything to Him, leaning into His presence, knowing that He had the power to exonerate me.

I joined a women's group that started a book series on "God of Creation." I attended and participated in the study, even though I was not acquainted with the members. This study was a life-changing experience for me. Through the weekly lessons and assignments, the Lord ministered to me and brought forth comfort and healing. I was empowered and determined to seek after God, without reservation.

After the women's study series ended, I joined a small group, where I was challenged to venture deeper into the Word of God. A profound transformation took place in my life. I reached a point where I started to examine my environments, my friends, and from whom I took counsel. During this process, the Lord was healing me spiritually, emotionally, mentally, and physically. The Lord told me, "It is okay to be vulnerable. I have placed you in a safe place." I was learning to trust again, although it was difficult to open up to my group about what I was dealing with. I was still healing from lost friendships, betrayal, and heartbreak. As I start attending a new church, there were things I needed to let go of from the old church, so I could be renewed in the new church. Letting go and deciding how, and with whom, to be vulnerable in a new environment was a process. Being in the small group was helping me to work through all that pain that I was feeling. The love I felt in this small group superseded anything I had ever experienced in past churches. They encouraged and prayed with me on a consistent basis. This small group was such a blessing, and it gave me hope that there were still people who cared about the hurting.

As mentioned earlier in this book, I have been through betrayal, abuse, misuse, deception, heartbreak, pain, hurt, health issues, and even car accidents, but I can say that, through it all, I am still standing, and I am learning to trust God. The Lord declares in his Word that He will never leave us nor forsake us (Hebrews 13:5b KJV). I am a living testimony, because even in my darkest moments, the Lord continues to reassure me that He is with me. I hold on to those words, even when I do not see a way out or even believe I can survive what I am going through. Today, I can declare that I am a restored woman of God. *"But as for you, you meant evil against me; but God meant it for my good, in order to bring it about as it is this day, to save many people alive"* (Genesis 50:20 NKJV).

When faced with obstacles and trials that seem unbearable, we often ask, "Why me, Lord?" But sometimes we go through trials and tribulations so God can birth what He has placed within us. Do not get me wrong, sometimes we are faced with trials and tribulations based on our own disobedience or the choices we made. Yes, that was what happened to me. Some things I encountered in my life were consequences of direct disobedience to the will of God for my life. I made choices that were outside the realm of the spirit. I have learned that it is important to pray and ask for God's directions before making decisions about our lives. I used to think that praying for direction was cliché. However, I have come to realize that it is not cliché. No matter how simple the matter we are presented with, we should pray for direction, because only God can see the future. At this stage of my life, I am endeavouring to pray about everything, no matter how simple it may seem. I have been through too many trials and tribulations to take things lightly. No, at this stage of my life, I cannot afford to repeat the mistakes of the past.

When the Lord impressed upon me to share my testimony in the form of a book, I was not excited at all. As I went through the process of writing, I wanted to give up on more than one occasion. There were times I questioned God, "Why me? I do not want to put my life out there for the world to see." I did not have a clue what restoration looked like on my own journey to even begin penciling my journey to share. The excerpt below is from one of my journal entries about my feelings and thoughts as I pushed forward in writing this book.

EXCERPT FROM JOURNAL ENTRY JULY 31, 2018

> *"Father, give me the strength to hold on and trust the process. Thinking about writing my testimony and the outcome of what restoration in my life looks like makes me feel scared in going forward. I know this is something I need to do, but I am feeling very nervous right now. But I must hold on to the Word of God that He will perfect that which concerns me.*
>
> *God, you impressed on my heart to write this testimonial, so I must push forward*

in faith, believing that when I reach the restoration section, you will reveal to me what restoration looks like in my life. I know it is well, and you are working on my behalf, and I just have to trust you wholeheartedly.

It is not over until God says it is. It is well, and this testimony will be completed, and it will minster and bring hope to women who are seeking answers for their lives, and will help them navigate their life through hard situations and circumstances.

I am E.L.L.A. – Empowered, Leader, Lovely, Affirmed. I am moving forward in what I believe God has placed in my heart. He has given me E.L.L.A to reach teenage girls, and He is healing me while I write my testimony.

So the way I see it now, I don't worry anymore as to what restoration looks like in my life, because I am already restored, and everything will fall into place. My confidence and faith are in God. It is well, and I just need to keep telling myself it is well, until it sinks deep into my spirit and becomes my motto."

Today I am not married, and I do not have children. However, that does not affect my restoration process.

I am restored by the blood of Jesus. God has sent His only begotten Son, whom He loves very much, to die on Calvary's cross so that my sins might be forgiven. Today I walk in total restoration as a child of the Most High God. Sometimes we look to our marital status to define who we are as a person. However, none of that determines if we are whole or walking in full restoration with God. When we are broken and seek God in our singleness, we tend to feel like not being married and not having children takes away from our lives. Yes, I would like to get married and have children, but I will leave that part of my life's journey in God's hands. With God all things are possible. For now, I am focusing on the restorative process. Restoration comes from God. When He restores, He provides a clean slate. Restoration is bringing me back to what God wants in my life. God is not like humans; He does not use our issues to judge us. When we seek Him and are restored, He does not see us through the lens of our past failures, issues, or negative tendencies.

God is healing my heart, restoring my faith, and giving me joy, peace, strength, and hope. I am reminded of the story of Ruth, how God restored her and gave her favour in the sight of Boaz. I know the Lord will reward me for my sufferings, my broken heart, and for the abuse, lies, and betrayals I have suffered. I have seen God at work, and His restoration is playing out in my life daily. I am a restored woman of God. I am anointed, called, God-fearing, smart, beautiful, intelligent, bold, confident, loving, trustworthy, faithful, kind, helpful, courageous, honourable, loyal, and gifted. The Lord has restored me with indescribable peace within and joy that I cannot even find the words to describe.

EXCERPT FROM JOURNAL ENTRY MAY 18, 2018

> *"Still I Rise"*
> *I am worthy of all God has for me.*
> *I am worthy to be loved.*
> *I am worthy to be cherished.*
> *I am blessed and highly favoured.*
> *God has good things in store for me.*
> *I am a child of God.*
> *I rise above every failed relationship.*
> *I rise above every heart break.*
> *I rise above every defeat.*
> *I rise above every feeling that I am not good enough.*
> *I rise above every feeling that I am not worthy to be loved.*
> *I rise above every feeling that something is wrong with me because I am single and not married with children.*
> *I rise above every feeling of failure.*
> *I will move forward in God, knowing that He holds me in the palm of His hands.*
> *I will move forward in faith.*
> *I will arise with my head lifted high, knowing I am a woman of God.*

As a part of my journey to restoration, the Lord asked me to pray for a particular individual who had broken my heart. It was something that I was not willing to do, but, in obedience to the Holy Spirit, I prayed for this individual based on how the Lord was directing me. I prayed on a consistent basis, until I felt a release in my spirit. Now I look back at that process and realize that the Lord was using it to bring healing and restoration to my life. I knew that for me to be truly healed I had to forgive everyone who caused me harm. I needed to let them go and surrender them to God. Don't get me wrong, I will never perceive them in the same manner as before, but I must remember that they are souls in need of Jesus' care. Forgiveness does not mean forgetting things that happened in our lives. Part of forgiving and valuing ourselves is creating healthy boundaries to safeguard ourselves and protect us from reliving the same experience. It is also about the freedom to live life unhindered by the past and to open our hearts to love fully the soul that God chooses to bring into our lives in the future.

As I reflect on everything that I have gone through, Matthew 6:33 echoes deeply in my heart: *"But seek first the Kingdom of God, and His righteousness and all these things shall be added to you."* In the year 2018, I experienced turmoil, betrayal, hurt, pain, and sickness that should have taken me out, but that verse has helped me to focus on what really matters. It teaches me not to be consumed with worldly things, but rather to chase after God. Chasing after God has proven to me that God takes care of His children. God is the sustainer, and He is amazing. I am learning to live a life that is pleasing to Him. Hebrews 11:6b (NKJV) states, *"God is a rewarder of them that diligently seek him."* Seeking God diligently has turned my life around in a tremendous way. He has placed people in my life that have been a blessing to me. I learned during this journey how to have a deeper trust in God and how to lean on His faithfulness. God is a restorer! I am determined to walk in the blessing of God and to continue on the path of restoration in all aspects of my life.

I don't know how my story will end, but what I do know is that it is well.

MY LIFE LESSONS

- Healing is achieved by addressing the source, not the symptom — Through my faith journey, God has healed my emotions and my expectations.
- Trust the process the Lord is taking you through — When the Lord said to me on February 18th, "Separate yourself; it is well," I had to put aside all my doubts and fears, and learn to trust the process daily, even though I didn't understand it and wanted to give up.
- Choose to believe what the Word of God declares over your life — Throughout this journey, my circumstances at times have been misleading, but I choose to believe that there is better ahead of me than what I endured and left behind me.
- Reset your expectations — When God gives us glimpses of what He has for us, we tend to fill in the blanks and over-analyze how we will get from where we are to where God is showing us. We must continually reset our daily expectations to come into alignment with what God is showing us to do.

REFLECTION

1. Have you fully surrendered yourself, your dreams, and your aspirations to the sovereign will of God?
2. What areas of your life are you believing God to restore?
3. Have you reset your expectations of what your restoration may or may not look like?

PRAYER

Heavenly Father, you are a loving and gracious God. You have been there through my sleepless nights, my tears, my pain, my broken heart. You never leave me nor forsake me, even when I cannot feel your presence. Thank you for your healing power that restores with joy unspeakable and peace that lives within me. *"Instead of your shame you will receive a double portion, and instead of disgrace you will rejoice in your inheritance. And so, you will inherit a double portion in your land, and everlasting joy will be yours"* (Isaiah 61:7 NIV), in Jesus' name. Amen.

ABOUT THE AUTHOR

Stacey-Ann Spence is a graduate of Seneca College of Applied Arts and Technology, The Humber Institute of Technology and Advanced Learning, and Ryerson University. Stacey-Ann started her career as an Administrator in 2000. After receiving her certification in Payroll, she worked as a Payroll and Benefits Administrator. Having completed her degree in Child and Youth Practitioner, she currently works as an Educational Intervenor. Stacey-Ann is the founder of E.L.L.A. (Empowered, Leader, Lovely, Affirmed), which was recently launched to encourage and empower young adolescent females. She currently resides in Bradford, Ontario, Canada.

www.ingramcontent.com/pod-product-compliance
Lightning Source LLC
LaVergne TN
LVHW041713060526
838201LV00043B/711